Kids' Klangers

summersdale

KIDS' KLANGERS

Illustrations by Milla Roelofse and Rob Melhuish

Summersdale Publishers Ltd
46 West Street
Chichester
West Sussex
PO19 1RP
UK

www.summersdale.com

Printed and bound in Great Britain

ISBN: 978-1-84953-096-5

Substantial discounts on bulk quantities of Summersdale books are available to corporations, professional associations and other organisations. For details contact Summersdale Publishers by telephone: +44 (0) 1243 771107, fax: +44 (0) 1243 786300 or email: nicky@summersdale.com.

Kids' klangers

The Funny Things That Children Say

Richard Benson

Contents

Introduction

Few people would deny that children really do say the funniest things. Sometimes it's a case of misquoting something they've heard at school, like 'I've been told I can take violence lessons in my music class', and other times it's a brilliant demonstration of innocent but completely accurate logic: 'Have you seen my favourite gloves? They are stripy, and they are shaped like my hand.'

There can be no doubt that having small children in your life can make you see the world in an altogether more interesting way, and this collection of charming and hilarious observations will make you remember just how much fun you had when you were still in short trousers!

Out and About

When passing a racetrack in the car:
Child:

What goes on there?

Parent:

It's where people race horses.

Child (after some thought):

I bet the horses win.

Girl:

Can I go and play with those boys outside?

Mother:

No, you can't, they're a bit rough when they play.

Girl:

But if I find a smooth one, can I play with him?

Mum at a toddler group to her small child when she spies some other mums looking her way:

I think my ears are burning.

Child (looking anxiously at her mum):

Quickly, put them out then!

Sweet-looking little girl says to colourful caterpillar found on the ground:

Aw, lovely little caterpillar... (stamps on it) THERE! You're dead now!

Child:

Daddy, I really need the toilet!

Dad:

OK, we'll stop soon. Do you need a number one or a number two?

Child (thinks about it for a while):

I need a twelve!

On seeing a headless tailor's
dummy in a clothes shop:

I'll pray for you.

About a house that only had the
wooden framing done:

Oh, I wouldn't want to live in
a house like that – it's naked!

Daddy, if you close your eyes when you drive, it makes you go faster!

Little Girl watching her father fall over as he tries to demonstrate how to roller-skate:

Mummy, what's Daddy doing now?

On the way out of an expensive shop, and in a loud voice:

Mummy, are we leaving because you don't have enough money to buy anything?

I went to Kenya for my holidays. I went not to have a safari adventure, but a family one. We went because all my family lives there... except my mum, dad, my brother, me and my sister.

On seeing a sign for no dog fouling:

What does that sign mean?
No smoking for dogs?

On seeing a dark line in the sea
from the plane window:

Look Mum, there's the EQUATOR!

Seeing a police dog in the
back of a police car:

What did he do?

When going into the toilet block
at an amusement park:

What ride is this, Mum?

About the GPS system in the car:

How does she know where
we are going?

Parent:

Look at that lovely German shepherd over there.

Child:

How do you know he's German?

To a bobby on the beat:
Oh my gosh, does your mum have to help you put those big boots on?

A little girl had wet her knickers and been told by her mother not to worry because it's just an accident. The next week while out shopping, she turns to her mummy and says:

I really need an accident!

Mum, I want to go on a cargo ship, you know, one that the car goes on!

A father and child were in an antiques shop looking at teddy bears. The dad had a bear at home from his childhood called William that was badly showing its age. The small child, being aware of the threadbare state of the bear goes up to the very snooty saleswoman and says in an earnest voice:

My daddy's Willy is going tufty.

When seeing people riding bicycles:
Don't their feet get dizzy?

For my holidays I went to Euroland and met Snow Wipe and Sleepy Booby. I met Mickey Mouse – he is a real mouse.

A mother and small child were at the funfair. The child is delighted with his mum's efforts on the 'Hook a Duck' stall and shouts with pride:

My mum is the best hooker!

I paid for my sweets myself. I went up to the lady and she put my pennies in her castrator.

After seeing their first
ever ballet performance:

Why were they on tiptoe all the time?
It would have been easier if they
just used taller people.

I'm not going in the car with Dad
– he drives like a ninny.

Pointing at a gravestone:

Mummy, do people live in there?

When I Grow Up

I would like to be a cow or a girl when I grow up.

When I'm big, if I have a baby and it's a boy, I'm going to have to sell it, because boys are really horrible!

I'm going to be a superhero and save the world. I'm going to go and do 1,000 push-ups in my room now.

I think I want to be a dragonfly when I grow up. Or a dentist.

I want to be just like my daddy when I get big, but not with so much hair all over. I'll probably have hair on my bottom just like my dad, too.

I want to be a teacher because I want to be allowed to wear high heels all day.

When I grow up I want a really massive house with spider legs.

I want to be a policeman, so I can arrest my daddy when he puts me on the naughty step.

I want to be a penguin so I can play outside all day.

I want to work with commuters because I'm good at pressing buttons.

Child:

I want to be a pirate when I grow up so I can fly the plane to Disney World and meet Mickey Mouse.

Parent:

It's a pilot that flies a plane, is that what you mean?

Child:

Can pilots wear eye patches and peg legs too?

I want to be a fish except I've never seen one. Do people eat fish?

I want to be a celebrity chef like Gordon Brown.

When I grow up I'm going to shave my arm pips.

I'm not sure if I want to grow up. Will my bones fall out like my teeth, so that bigger ones can grow?

Animals and Pets

Make sure that you never blow in a cat's ear because if you do, usually after three or four times, they will bite your lips together! And they don't let go for at least a minute.

Electric eels can give you a shock.
They live in caves under the sea where
I think they have to plug themselves
into chargers.

A dolphin breathes through its bottom on the top of its face.

Sharks are ugly and mean and have big teeth, just like my big sister. She's not my friend any more.

My parents took me to the zoo at the weekend. My favourite animal is a fricken elephant.

Child:

Dad! I think our cat is dead!

Dad:

How do you know that?

Child:

Because I pissed in its ear.

Dad:

YOU DID WHAT??

Child:

You know... I bent down and went pssssst in its ear and it didn't move.

Why do cow yards smell like poo?
Don't they know how to flush?

A little girl's puppy wanders into the bathroom when she's in the bath.

Girl:

No Mum, he can't come in!

Mum:

Why? He's only a little puppy dog.

Girl:

But he's a BOY puppy!
And I'm naked in here.

Did God mean for giraffes to look like that or was it an accident?

My puppy still has stinky breath even after I gave her a Polo mint.

A preschooler speaks to his dad about some newborn kittens that he went to see with his mum:

Boy:

There were two boy kittens and one girl.

Dad:

How could you tell?

Boy:

Well, the woman who owns them picked them up and looked underneath – I think it's printed on their bottoms.

I saw a hedgehog and
it had pickles all over it.

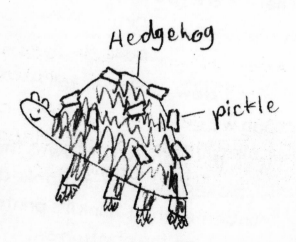

Hedgehog

pickle

Never wear yellow outside because bees and wasps will chase you. They think you're a dandelion.

A small child when collecting eggs in the morning from the family's chickens:

Can we get some pigs, then I can collect the bacon and sausages in the morning too?

Crabs can hurt because they have little princes that can nip you.

We went to a farm and the farmer pointed out his prize bollock. It was really big and steam was coming off it because it was a cold day.

My dad taught me about lemons. They jump off cliffs to their deaths. I would not like to be a lemon.

My Family

Little girl threatening younger sister:

If you're going to do that, you'll have to face the quenchy-quenchies!

My mummy is the best, and I love her so much that as soon as she's dead I'm going to bury her underneath my bedroom window.

Two children overheard in the playground discussing what their parents do for a living.

First child:

My dad is a postman and
my mum is a teacher.

Second child:

My dad is an old codger – at least
that's what my mum says he is, but I'm
sure what one of those is.

Whenever your mum is angry and asks you, 'Do I look stupid?' it's always best not to answer her.

Mummy, when you're dead, can I have your slippers?

Don't let your mum brush your hair
when she's in a bad mood
with your dad.

Always ask your grandparents for
something if your mum and
dad have said no first.

Why don't grandma and grandpa have names like the rest of us?

A grandfather is a man-grandmother.

A little boy after seeing an ultrasound:

My mummy is having a baby. I know because I saw it on the telly!

On seeing grandma's false teeth in a glass by the side of the bed:

I can't believe it! How much is she going to get from the tooth fairy for all of those?

A child after seeing his parents'
wedding photos:

Is that when Mummy came
to work for us?

Small child to grandma:

Are you older than my other nana?
Does that mean you'll die first?

I'm glad you're not deaf, Grandma.
Because then you wouldn't hear
the funny things that I say.

My dad taught me that you must only
use swear words when
using a hammer.

My mum told me she is stagnant,
I hope I get a baby sister.

Indignant child to their grandmother
after being told off:

Well I don't care what you say,
because every night you sleep next to
my granddad and cuddle up
to him like a big wimp!

Sunday School

God spoke to me one night. He said 'Rmmrrm!' But it might have been a lawn mower or a motorbike.

What did God stand on when he was creating the Earth?

I am not really a Christian.
I believe in fairies and pixies.

Child (pointing to a dead bird in the garden):

Daddy, what happened to him?

Dad:

He died and went to heaven.

Child:

Did God throw him back down?

Angels don't eat but they
drink milk from holy cows.

Sunday school teacher:

And why is it necessary
to be quiet in church?

Child:

Because people are sleeping.

The Bible says that God made light.
But we were told in school that
Thomas Edison made it.
Did he steal God's idea?

Three children were conducting a makeshift funeral for their newly departed pet hamster. After a rousing rendition of 'All Things Bright and Beautiful', the oldest child, acting as the vicar, intoned,

'In the name of the Father, and of the Son and *in the hole he goes.*'

Angels look after your pets when they are sick. And if the animals don't get better, they help the child get over it.

Child:

God! God! GOD!

Mum:

What's the matter?

Child:

I'm just talking to God. Why isn't he talking back to me?

Our Father, Who does art in heaven, Harold is His name.

And lead us not into temptation,
but deliver us some email.

Child:

Grandma, do you know how
you and God are alike?

Grandmother:

No, how are we alike?

Child:

You're both really old.

God looks after us when we are sleeping because he has a special key and just lets himself in.

The seventh commandment is thou shalt not admit adultery.

The greatest miracle in the Bible is when Joshua told his son to stand still and he obeyed him.

A small child was looking at an old Bible in his parents' house and very carefully turning the fragile pages. Someone had used the book as a flower press at one time and out fell a few leaves and flower heads. The stunned child shouted to his mum:

Look! I think I've found Adam and Eve's underwear!

It was a miracle when Jesus rose from the dead and managed to get the tombstone off the entrance.

Jesus was born because Mary had an immaculate contraption.

Angels live in cloud houses made by God and his son, who's a very good carpenter.

After a wrong number:

Mum, who was on the phone? Was it Jesus?

When we go to heaven we get to live with Santa and Rudolph in the sky. That's where my hamster went.

Angels work for God and look after
all the children when God is
busy with other things.

Looking at headstones in a cemetery:

Are those the Ten Commandments?

Overheard in church:

Oh come let us ignore him
Oh come let us ignore him
Oh come let us ignore him
Price that lawn.

God created Adam and Ebay.

God is really old and wrinkly,
kind of like a dinosaur He-Man.

A small child to a shocked mother on
the way home from school:

Milly and Jane said that their parents
are Roman Catholic, so I told them
that our family are all prostitutes.

Today I learned about doughnut and the whale in Sunday school – doughnut was eaten by the whale because he'd been bad. He was a bad doughnut.

A small child and his father are standing at the entrance to the church after matins and are looking at a war memorial.

Child:

Daddy, what's that?

Dad:

It's a memorial that's dedicated to those who have died in service.

Child (wide-eyed):

What? The service this morning?

Dinner Time

On being told that sausages
are made from pigs:

You can't eat pigs – they're
the farmer's pets!

I have chocolate flavour milk at
bedtime. And Molly (pointing to her
baby sister) has booby flavour.

I think beer must be good. My dad says the more beer he drinks, the prettier my mummy looks.

Can I have sprinklers on my ice cream?

A boy opens a box of animal-shaped biscuits and empties them out all over the kitchen table:

Mum:

What on earth are you doing?

Child:

It says on the box that you shouldn't eat them if the seal is broken. I'm trying to find the seal.

My mum's a virgin because she doesn't eat meat.

Child after having a piece of popcorn extracted from his ear:
Doctor

Why did you put the popcorn in your ear?

Child:

I didn't put it in there...
my ear sucked it up!

If turkey comes from turkeys, does ham come from hamsters?

I love toucans on my soup. They're really crunchy but also a bit chewy and get stuck in my teeth.

Explaining the difference between
an item of food and a dish:

A carrot is a carrot,
but macaroni cheese isn't.

Mummy, long ago, did you have food?

On seeing sesame seeds
on a burger bun:

This has hamburger seeds in it!

After having some microwave beans:

That's the best meal you've
ever made me!

I used to believe that when I ate all my dinner up that it went down to my toes. Now I know it only reaches my knees.

Before people landed on the moon, everyone thought the moon was made of cheese. It's actually made of rock, but that's what happens to cheese when you leave it out of the fridge for too long.

Asked if they've had chicken pox:

No, but I've had Cocoa Pops.

Small child when asked what
their favourite vegetable is:

Chocolate!

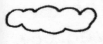

I love going to the cinema
and having cop porn.

Being green means eating more orgasmic vegetables, because they're better for you.

I'm not having grilled cheese sandwiches. Boys only eat boy cheese sandwiches!

That was spicy. It hurt my feelings.

Small child when asked why they
are not eating their dinner:

I've lost my apple tights.

A small child was helping to bake a cake.
After breaking the eggs and eyeing
up the electric whisk she says:

Can I make the eggs dizzy now?

Small child who has eaten too much:

Mummy, my cheese is biting back!

My dad isn't very well today
because of his overhang.

School Days

When Robert brought his Action Man into school it was constipated, because we're not allowed to have toys in school.

Who draws the lines around the countries?

A fossil is something really old.
It sometimes contains the
footprints of a fish.

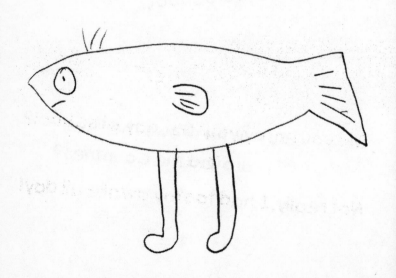

Elbow grease is what you use to make things clean. You can only use it when you have a scab on your elbow, otherwise there's no grease.

Dad:

Did you enjoy your first day at school?

Child:

Not really, I had to stay awake all day!

We've got a spinach girl coming to stay. I won't know what to say to her, though, because I don't know spinach.

I learned how to do colouring-in in deception class today.

We made a leaving card for Mrs Bow because she is retarded at the end of term.

If you are surrounded by sea you are an island. If you don't have sea all around you, you are incontinent.

When teachers get old, like over
forty, they're always in
a really grumpy mood.

In a geography class:
Thunder is a rich source of loudness.

Most of the houses in France are made of plaster of Paris.

It used to be Mummy who took me to school, but now we have a big new bust that takes us.

A buzzard is when it snows sideways, but tomatoes are even more dangerous – you can see them coming from miles off and they can wreck houses and lift cars off the ground.

You can listen to thunder after lightning and tell how close you came to getting hit. If you don't hear it you got hit.

Talc is found on rocks and on babies.

I've been told I can take violence lessons in my music class, except I'd rather play the piano.

Christmas

The three wise men brought the baby Jesus some presents of gold, frankincense, myrrh and silver. But I think he would have preferred some Star Wars action figures.

There was an angel at Jesus' birth called Gabriel. All he did was fly around a lot.

I think Jesus was born in a shed, or a barn, or a stable – one of the three.

They followed a special Christmas star, which is only out in December.

Jesus's mummy and daddy are called Jovis and Mary.

Is the Frankie Scents
like men's perfume?

A small child when inside a
church for a carol service:

Where's Carol then?

After counting down to one we all shouted happy new ear.

Overexcited child on Christmas Eve, while putting out a mince pie and sherry for Father Christmas:

Oh I know – why don't we leave him half the turkey as well?!

The Birds and the Bees

When are you going to tell me about the birds and the Bee Gees?

Love is what happens when a girl puts on perfume and a boy puts on aftershave and they go out together and smell each other.

Child:

Is your belly button a door that your baby comes out of?

Mum:

No.

Child:

Phew, because that would really hurt!

When you love somebody, your eyelashes go up and down and little stars and rainbows come out of you.

A small child asking about
how babies are made:

How do you find the bones for them?
Are they lying around somewhere?

If we started life as a tadpole why am I not a frog? It's not fair.

A child talking about his baby brother:

First, Mum and Dad made him as a symbol of their love, and then Dad put a seed in Mum's stomach, and he grew in there. He ate for nine months through an umbrella cord.

Will I lay eggs when I'm a grown-up?

When asked what a midwife does:

She delivers babies, but she doesn't have a sign on the car like the Domino's man.

I'm not sure how the egg gets there to begin with, but I think it comes from food. You have to eat very healthy food, even like eighteen broccolis a week.

How are mothers made?

God made my mum just the same like he made me. He just used bigger parts.

What Do You Look Like?

My grandma is a very nice lady but her skin doesn't fit her face.

To a cashier:

You have such lovely yellow teeth.

Mum! Daddy's hair is missing off the top of his head!

Small child to grandma:

You look like a very pretty man.

Mummy, I'm sure you were taller last year.

Small child to sweaty daddy:

Why is your face leaking?

Child:

Mum, you've got boobies.

Mother:

Yes, I have.

Child:

All mums have got boobies haven't they?

Mother:

Yes...

Child:

Why has daddy got them then?

Mother, on seeing her child
with food round her face:
Just look at your face! To which the
confused child cries: I can't!

My baby sister looks like a volcano
about to burst when she has wind.

Small child pointing to a woman in a cafe:

Mummy, do all women grow moustaches?

Mum, you'd look so much better if you rubbed out those lines on your face.

Child on seeing his mum
applying make-up:

Why are you drawing round your eyes?
Is it so you don't lose them?

What Love is All About

On seeing a couple kissing:

He seems to be whispering
in her mouth.

If grown-ups are in love, they are
all dressed up. And if they are just
wearing jeans and a T-shirt it might
mean they just broke up.

I'm worried about what will happen with my bed when I get married. How will I fit my wife in?

If you're not wearing your ring, someone else might try and steal you!

When a person falls in love for the first time, they fall over, and they don't get up for at least an hour. It can really hurt!

If falling in love is as hard as learning how to write, I don't want to do it.

Make sure you're good at kissing by the time you get married, so your wife won't mind if you never do the washing up.

Married people always hold hands when walking down the street to make sure their rings don't fall off, because they were very expensive.

My mum says it's best to find someone who is kind. That's what I'll do. I'll find somebody who's kinda tall and kinda handsome.

When people get married they promise to go through sickness and diseases together.

If it's your mother, you can kiss her whenever you like. But if it's someone new, you must ask them first.

Marriage is when you get to keep your girl and don't have to give her back to her parents.

On seeing a couple kissing:

I think he's trying to steal her lunch!

Home Time

Mum:

Is that a party invitation?

Child:

Yes, but I can't go because it says 2 to 4 on it and I'm 5.

While watching TV with her mum, a child passes the remote control and says:

Here you go, Mum. You can be Daddy.

A mum was feeling a bit tearful after a hard day looking after her two small children. One child says to the dad who has just walked in:

Is she teething?

I love watching the adverts. My favourite is the one with the Durex doggy.

A little boy keeps on playing with his willy in the bath, so his mum tells him not to play with it or it might fall off, to which he replies:

What, like yours has?

Have you seen my favourite gloves? They are stripy, and they are shaped like my hand.

Will you play hide and seek with me?
I'm going to hide under my bed,
so don't look there.

Parent:

Why are you not replying to me?

Child:

My face is asleep, be quiet!

Frustrated with a childproof cap:

How does it know it's me?

Small child on being told her
friend had broken her arm:

What, right off?

Can we watch Star Tracks?
I love Jean Luc B'stard.

When asked what they would do if
there were no parents:

We could eat chocolate cake
whenever we wanted to!

American child to English babysitter:

I wanna go potty.

English babysitter (misunderstanding):

Oh you want to go to a party? Parties *are* fun, aren't they?

Child:

I wanna go potty!

Babysitter:

Yes but we have to go and meet your parents now sweetheart.

Child (rolls eyes and sighs with exasperation):

No silly, I gotta go to the bathroom!

Child:

I can't sleep because there's a monster under my bed.

Mum:

Don't be silly, it's just your imagination.

Child:

What's my imagination doing under there?

Mum:

You did a brilliant job of putting your sandals on except they are on the wrong feet.

Child:

But I don't have any other feet, Mum.

Showing her mum a rash:

Look Mum, I've got heat raddish!

Little girl called Grace:

Hail Mary, full of Suzanne...

Mother:

No, it's 'full of grace'.

Grace:

I know, but I thought my sister might like a turn at having her own special prayer named after her!

Dad:

I'm going to teach you about building a fire – do you know what you can burn on a fire?

Child:

Wood and paper.

Dad:

That's right – and what about coal?

Child:

What, like Cheryl Cole?

← Cole

After falling out of bed:

I wasn't watching where
I was sleeping.

A parent calls home and after a few
rings their child answers:

Hello.

Parent:

Gosh, you sound out of breath.

Child:

No, I have more.

A little girl had a pet tabby cat called Alice.
One day she saw a strange white
cat in the garden and said:

Look Mummy, there's a
white Alice outside!

A penny for your socks, Dad.

Child:

Mum, I want an 'orse.

Mum:

You want a horse?!

Child:

No I want oars to row my boat with.

On being told to behave:

I am being have!

Have you enjoyed this book?

If so, why not write a review on
your favourite website?

Thanks very much for buying
this Summersdale book.

www.summersdale.com